Any Given Someday

The Poetry Of What Comes Next

John Roedel

Copyright © 2018 by **John Roedel**

All rights reserved. No part of this publication may be reproduced, distributed or transmitted in any form or by any means, without prior written permission.

John Roedel

Heygodheyjohn.com

Publisher's Note: This is a work of fiction. Names, characters, places, and incidents are a product of the author's imagination. Locales and public names are sometimes used for atmospheric purposes. Any resemblance to actual people, living or dead, or to businesses, companies, events, institutions, or locales is completely coincidental.

Book Layout © 2017 BookDesignTemplates.com

Any Given Someday/ John Roedel. -- 1st ed.
ISBN-13: 978-1791382421

For my dad.

He would have loved this.

Someday we will both be ghosts together.
Imagine all the adventures we'll have.

Aside from the names of my children, there is no other word that I tethered myself to more than the word "someday".

This word has served as my sidekick throughout my entire life. Someday is how I have chosen to answer most of the big questions that I have been asked during my time here on Earth.

The older I get, the more complicated the questions have gotten:

When am I going to finish my homework?" **Someday**.

When am I going to grow up? **Someday**.

When will I mow the lawn? **Someday**.

ANY GIVEN SOMEDAY

When will I figure out what I want to do with my life?
Someday.

When will I stop letting depression control my life?   **Someday**

When will I let go of my past mistakes?
Someday.

When will I forgive those who gave me my scars?
Someday.

When will I start looking for beauty in the world?
Someday.

When will I start to stand up for what I know is right?
Someday.

When will I believe in miracles again?
　Someday.

Ask me any question and my response is usually the same.

Someday. Someday. Someday.

I marvel at the fact that my liberal usage of the word during my day-to-day life hasn't caused my wife to take a bigger interest in daytime drinking. I have procrastinated my life away by hiding behind all my endless somedays. It was my way of saying "later" or "not yet" to situations life was inviting me to take a hard look at. It was the coward's way out for ever giving myself or the world a deadline for what I wanted to change.

I built my house with a million different *somedays* and it wasn't until recently that I noticed it was starting to crumble. What I have learned is that "**Someday**" isn't so far away. I can't go on putting off everything that I want to do with my life. I can't hide from the fact that our world is changing.

Things aren't a **someday** away.
Someday is now.
We can't ignore it anymore.
Someday is today.
Some of these entries give me hope.
Some of these entries haunt me.
Either way there is no more putting things off.

Someday is here.

I sure as hell hope we are ready for it.

ANY GIVEN SOMEDAY

> Someday my heart and my brain will form a really kick-ass band.

ANY GIVEN SOMEDAY

> Someday I'll prove that mercy sounds just like a softly played piano.

Someday the
   homeless won't make
      them so angry.

ANY GIVEN SOMEDAY

> Someday you will fit in and instantly regret it.

ANY GIVEN SOMEDAY

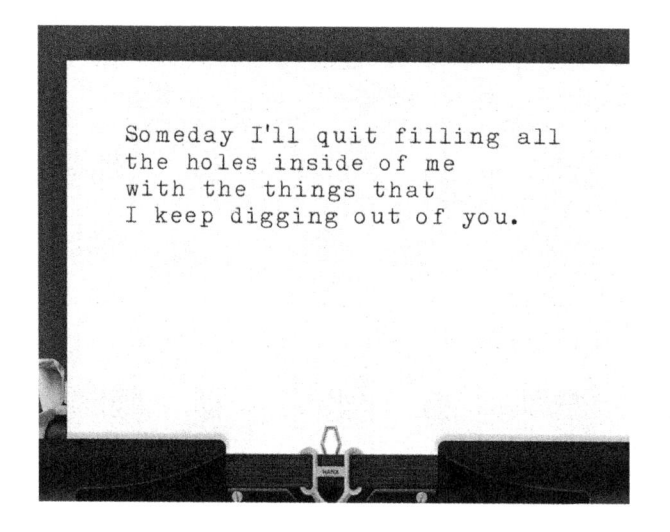

Someday I'll quit filling all
the holes inside of me
with the things that
I keep digging out of you.

ANY GIVEN SOMEDAY

Someday old people won't give a shit about what music young people are listening to.

ANY GIVEN SOMEDAY

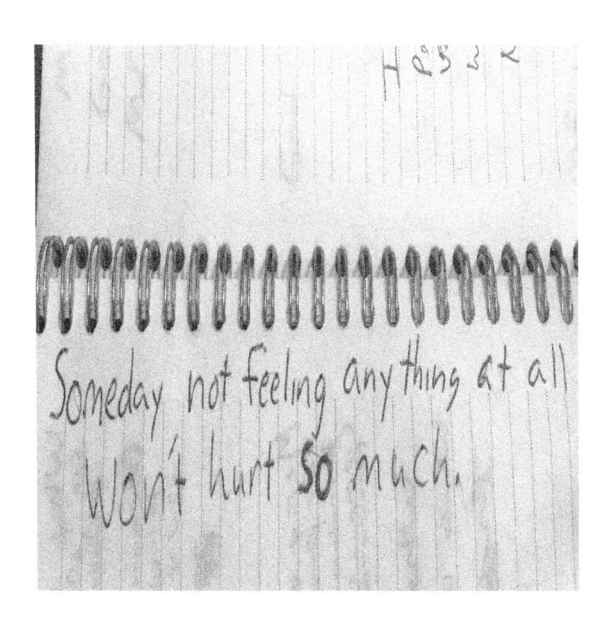

> Someday not feeling anything at all won't hurt so much.

ANY GIVEN SOMEDAY

> Someday you will finally believe that none of this is your fault.

Someday a scientist will thaw all your frozen tears and every single terrible word that I ever said to you will come back to life to eat us all.

ANY GIVEN SOMEDAY

Someday our schools will feel more like gardens.

Someday you will save a person's life by NOT trying to fix them.

ANY GIVEN SOMEDAY

> Someday a racist will be buried in flowers

worry lines

Someday everything that I think that I know will be torn apart by all the things that I never knew.

Someday we will all be guilty of something so maybe we should put down our pitchforks and torches and just go home and eat some cake?

Someday I will put you in a book that nobody will read.

Someday kindness will be our currency.

ANY GIVEN SOMEDAY

Someday you will have to climb the staircase to an ancient lighthouse to discover that the only way to turn its light back on is to forgive yourself.

Shadows hate mercy.

> Someday he will quit yelling at her long enough to discover that she has already been gone for years.

Someday we will be more afraid of violence than we are nudity.

ANY GIVEN SOMEDAY

> Someday Punching a Nazi will be an Olympic Sport.

ANY GIVEN SOMEDAY

Someday we will quit trying to domesticate our wildest dreams. Let them be feral and dirty and full of teeth and always lurking at the edge of the woods watching us with their wide ravenous eyes.

Don't you dare break your wild dreams. Let them run free and if we are both lucky, someday they will drag us both into the forest to be devoured by them.

Someday
Hope will
permanently
Stain us.

ANY GIVEN SOMEDAY

Someday we will invent
a word for a coward
who becomes more
than all their fears.

ANY GIVEN SOMEDAY

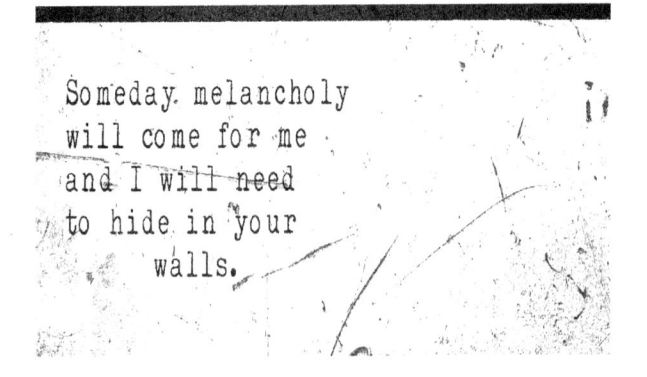

Someday melancholy
will come for me
and I will need
to hide in your
walls.

ANY GIVEN SOMEDAY

> Someday my kids won't "be something."
> Someday my kids will be SOMEBODY.

Someday we won't ask children "What do you want to be when you grow up?"

Instead we'll ask them, "What kind of miracle will your life be for other people?"

Maybe I'm biased. The more I think about it, I'm sure I am. When I was a kid nobody ever asked me what I wanted to be when I grew up.

ANY GIVEN SOMEDAY

Nobody knew what to do with me.
Not even my parents.
Not even me.
Maybe nobody ever thought I would grow up, so what's the point, right?

Now that I'm older
And untethered
And drifting
And aimless
And wandering
- no, not wandering.
Wandering isn't a strong enough
word for what has become of me.
I'm lost.
I never became anything.

Now that I'm older, untethered, drifting, lost and never became anything
- I'm so very tempted to badger
My children into worrying
About WHAT they are going to

be in twenty years.

I know that's what I'm supposed to do. Grey my hair over their ACT scores and bloviate at them for blowing a quiz on The War of 1812 - because how in the hell are they ever going to become a corporate lawyer if they get a C in history class?!

I think I'm meant to fret and yell at them more than I do.

The thing is…I can't. I'm more worried about who they are going to be all the time, rather than what they are going to be doing for eight hours a day when they are in their thirties.

If forced to choose, I'd rather have a child of mine live as a beggar who is covered in perspective and kindness than an asshole dermatologist who snaps at his waiter and forgets that we are all just specks of dust living on a bigger speck of dust flying through an expanding universe that appears to have no end.

The hope is that they land somewhere in between those two options. There is an elusive intersection where both inner-joy and material success meet. I've never found it myself, but I will leave them a map made of poetry written on napkins and loose paper that should help them begin their search for that sweet spot.

As a father of three boys I will mark my grade as a parent by how generous they become, and how they treat women and how seriously they won't take themselves and how much laughter they spread and how they give their hearts to people and how authentically they live their lives.

I sound like a hippie parent. Let me try and earn back some credibility with you. I want my kids to value their service to the world more than they do their 401Ks or which all-inclusive resort they will visit next.

That still sounds like something a hippie parent would say. I'll try to explain it in a different way:

Someday when my children are gathered around my gravestone, I pray that they will hold up a caramel colored glass of Irish whiskey and toast their unsuccessful father who never became something but always worked so hard to be somebody.

ANY GIVEN SOMEDAY

There is a difference between the two things.

Kids,
Don't be something.
Be somebody.
Somebody who is kind.
Somebody who is merciful.
Somebody who is unaffected by the expectations of other people.
Somebody who believed in
miracles so deeply
that they became one themselves.

Kids,
Just be yourselves.
I mean it.
Be
Authentically yourselves.
You each have
A body that under its skin
has a caldera of endless light
- That once it breaks through
will shoot forth an

ANY GIVEN SOMEDAY

Arc of light that can
Be seen from Venus.

Don't be something.
Be more than that.
Be a miracle.
Be you.

Locate the intersection
between joy and success.

When you find it, please plant a
row of wildflowers nearby
and name them after me.

ANY GIVEN SOMEDAY

SOMEDAY THE TWO OF US SHOULD

WRITE DOWN ALL OF OUR FEARS

TO MAKE SURE WE DON'T

HAVE THE SAME ONES.

THIS WAY ONE OF US WILL BE

BRAVE FOR THE OTHER ONE.

I CALL DIBS ON BEES.

ANY GIVEN SOMEDAY

> Someday I will need you.
> Please still be here.

Someday they will just call Autism by its real name: ***Courage.***

ANY GIVEN SOMEDAY

Someday I will quit wasting time counting your mistakes.

ANY GIVEN SOMEDAY

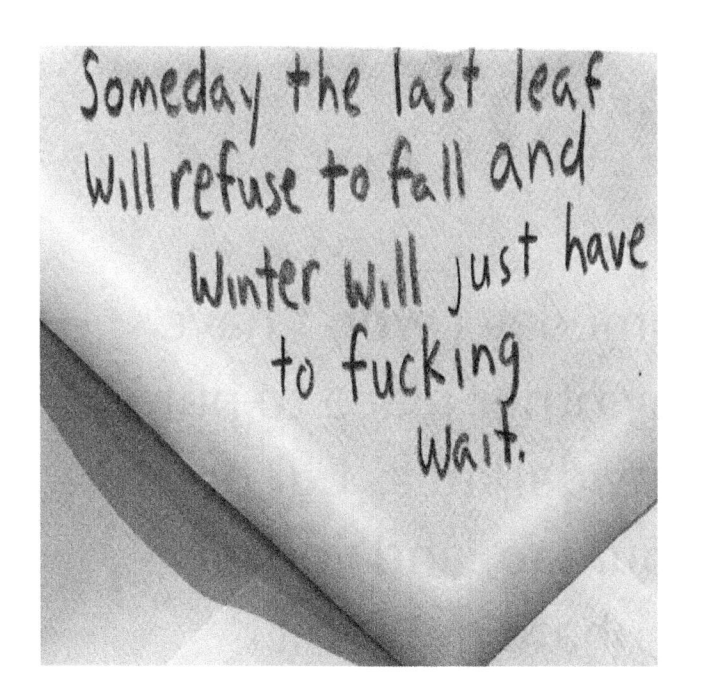

> Someday the last leaf will refuse to fall and winter will just have to fucking wait.

ANY GIVEN SOMEDAY

Someday I won't have any other place to put my darkness but on your lap, and you will hate me for it.

ANY GIVEN SOMEDAY

someday as I'm
dying in a white
little bed I will
close my eyes and
relive every single
kiss that you ever
gave me.

ANY GIVEN SOMEDAY

Someday you won't fold your arms while you talk to me.

Someday we will pass each other on the street as strangers who happen to know everything about each other.

ANY GIVEN SOMEDAY

> Someday an ounce of your courage will silence a ton of assholes

ANY GIVEN SOMEDAY

Someday a child will need you to believe them.

Someday a comet wipe out all life on Earth – but until that day you have no excuse to not be kind.

ANY GIVEN SOMEDAY

Someday I will be so locked up inside that I'll need you to let me out. I left a key under the mat. If it's not there check the windows, I usually leave them open during the springtime. If that doesn't work you may have to use an axe. Smash away. It's okay. I have been thinking that I am tired of living in a world with doors anyway. Rip them all down and come find me. I'll probably be on the floor in the kitchen. Drag me outside and I'll tell you where the matches are so we can burn this place down. I've made a home out of regret and I don't want to live here anymore. After that we will need a sacred place to bury all of the ashes. Sometimes they come back if you don't. Maybe you should just come and get me out now. The shadow people are back.

Did you find the key yet? Hurry.

ANY GIVEN SOMEDAY

> Someday aliens will discover your old diary and it will break their yellow hearts.

ANY GIVEN SOMEDAY

> Someday everything that I have buried will demand Headstones.

ANY GIVEN SOMEDAY

ANY GIVEN SOMEDAY

Someday I won't let my roots become my chains.

ANY GIVEN SOMEDAY

SOMEDAY WE WON'T CALL THE BOMBS WE DROP **"MOTHER"** ANYMORE.

Someday we will find a clever new nickname for the weapons we use. Calling a massive bomb that we drop from the sky a "Mother" seems counterintuitive.

I don't get it. We should only put the names of things that we want to erase from human history on the sides of bombs. Like Nickelback or Zima.

Mothers are vessels of life.
Bombs are destroyers.
There are no similarities between moms & bombs.
The former brings comfort and warmth. The latter brings fire and ash. One makes a family and the other separates them under rubble.

War is war.
Mothers are mothers.
Quit mixing ash and roses together

ANY GIVEN SOMEDAY

while asking me to smirk and high five my grocery clerk who is "finally proud of our country again" because we have torn the Earth in two with our Mother Of All Bombs.

My mom wasn't a bomb. She was a piece of tough Wyoming sagebrush. There wasn't a winter that ever scared her. She stood against the relentless wind without shuddering. Yes, she was so stubborn that even the dusty old west wind gusts couldn't make her sway. She stood proud and without allowing one branch of her family to break off during a storm.

My mom wasn't a bomb.
She could have been. She had the power to explode and blow the shit out of all of us with the ordinances she kept buried deep within her bunker - but she didn't.

My mom wasn't a bomb. But she could have been had she wanted to. She wasn't passive. She was the simmering volcano that could reform the world if she allowed herself to explode. She never did. She chose a different way.

My mom chose to shake the Earth
with her courage and her steadfast loyalty to those that

she gave her heart to. She had the choice to bring lives forward or to ruin them. She chose the garden over the slaughterhouse.

Mothers aren't bombs. They are sacrifice and unconditional love and worry lines and insomnia and hugs that squeeze us so hard that our souls start squeaking out of our ears.

Mothers don't belong on bombs. They belong on the magnificent rainbows above giant waterfalls. They are reflections of light and life. Mothers are the antithesis of bombs.

I'm not saying don't wage your fucking war.
Just leave mothers alone..
Leave my mom out of it.
She doesn't deserve to be on your bomb.
She deserves to be have her name etched on every shamrock in Ireland.
Can't you work on that instead?
Mothers aren't bombs.
They are our shelter.

ANY GIVEN SOMEDAY

> Someday a school shooting will be the last one.

ANY GIVEN SOMEDAY

Someday doubt will be considered a virtue.

ANY GIVEN SOMEDAY

Someday the moon will leave us for a better planet – but it won't matter because you will still light my nights and control my tides.

Someday
I'll be
a
cautionary
tale.

ANY GIVEN SOMEDAY

Someday every single powergrid will fail and we all will fall in love with sunrises again

ANY GIVEN SOMEDAY

Someday I'll be funny again.

ANY GIVEN SOMEDAY

> Someday a simple kiss will cut you in two

Someday depression won't feel so much like shame.

ANY GIVEN SOMEDAY

> Someday I will hold you in my thoughts and never let you out ever again.

ANY GIVEN SOMEDAY

Someday a
        robot will
        sit down
        next
        to you

                in church.

ANY GIVEN SOMEDAY

once there was

a forest that

was the home

to a little robin

one day

the little robin

asked God

"What song

would You like

me to sing for You?"

God responded to her

in a falling rose petal.

"Oh, my dear

little Robin, I love you

but don't sing Me a song."

The robin was confused.

"But I have so many songs

I could serenade You with.

ANY GIVEN SOMEDAY

I have a lovely ballad about the
sunrise that will make even You cry."

"That's okay, my little robin.
I don't want you to sing Me a song."
God said quietly to her through the breeze.

"God must not be able hear me correctly"
the little robin thought.

She then flew up to the
top of the highest tree in the park
and asked

"God, can I offer You a hymn
on how much I love my wings?
It is such a beautiful song."

God spoke to the little robin
through a single beam of sunlight.

"No, little robin, I
don't want you to
sing Me a song.

ANY GIVEN SOMEDAY

In fact, I don't want
you to sing a song
ever again."

The little heart
in the little robin
started to break.

She had been practicing her
whole life to become a beautiful
singer.
The little robin felt
so lost.

"But if I am not to sing,
what is my purpose?

God came down
to the little robin
in the form
of a single
drop of rain
that landed on her
tiny beak and said

ANY GIVEN SOMEDAY

"I don't want you to sing
a song.
I want you to become
a song."

Suddenly the little
robin felt a warmth
inside her that she
had never felt before.

It was peace.
It was peace.
It was purpose
It was peace.
It was a fire

the little robin
began to glow
and then just
like that she
split into four
equal pieces

ANY GIVEN SOMEDAY

the first piece was a falling rose petal
the second piece was a gentle breeze
the third piece was a radiating sunbeam
and the last piece was a single drop of rain
and it was all a song
and the little robin
became the most
beautiful song any
animal in the forest
had ever heard

Someday I will be a song!!!

ANY GIVEN SOMEDAY

Someday Joy.

Someday when you ask me for advice I will give you a song instead of a sermon.

ANY GIVEN SOMEDAY

> Someday you may have to lose your mind in order to save your heart.

Someday I want you to listen to The Pet Shop Boys and pretend that I'm still there dancing wildly next to you.

Someday it wont matter who won the war.

ANY GIVEN SOMEDAY

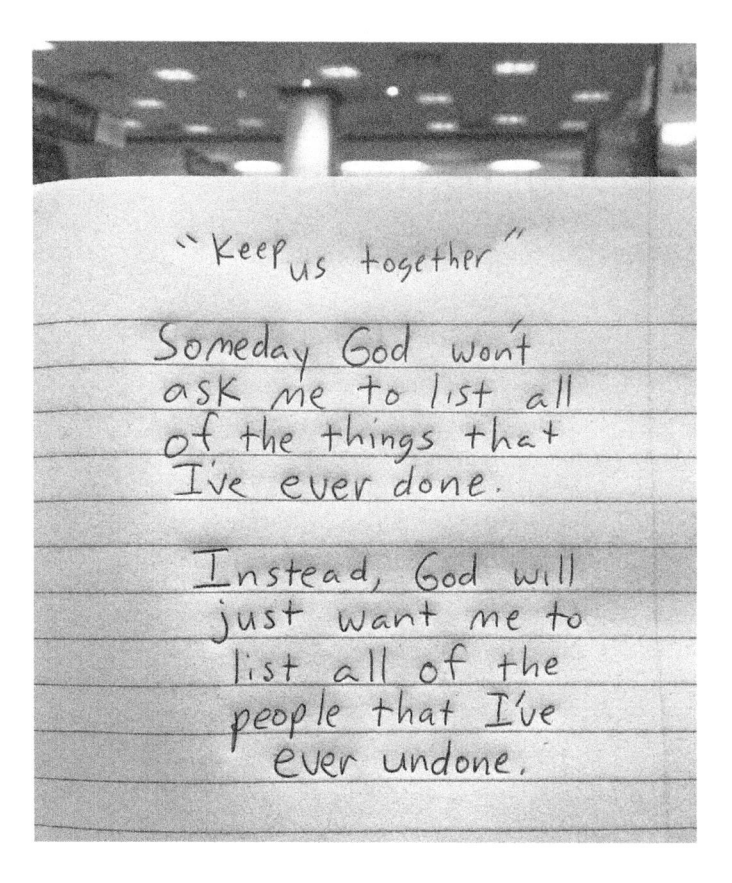

"Keep us together"

Someday God won't ask me to list all of the things that I've ever done.

Instead, God will just want me to list all of the people that I've ever undone.

ANY GIVEN SOMEDAY

Someday we will need a looooooonnnng wall to protect THEM from us

ANY GIVEN SOMEDAY

Someday we will meet for the first time and wonder why it took so long.

Someday you will fall in love and you'll never stop falling. You should know that if it's real love that you have fallen into then it will be an endless abyss. If it's love – and I'm talking REAL LOVE – you will keep falling and failing. Tumbling and tumbling. Down and down. Your feet will never touch the ground ever again. You'll be weightless.

ANY GIVEN SOMEDAY

Someday my life won't feel like I'm holding onto a

m
e
l
t
i
n
g

ice cube

ANY GIVEN SOMEDAY

Someday you will have to explain what a mushroom cloud is to a 3-year-old.

ANY GIVEN SOMEDAY

> **SOMEDAY A BULLY WILL BE AFRAID OF YOUR VOICE.**

ANY GIVEN SOMEDAY

Someday you
will unfriend me
and it will
be okay.
Really it will be.

ANY GIVEN SOMEDAY

Someday my mind will fail, and I will forget her name

and our story
and our children
and all our fights
and our vows
and our love

and she won't give a damn
she will love me like I'm still there
even though I have already gone

that is love
thatislove thatislove thatislove

ANY GIVEN SOMEDAY

ANY GIVEN SOMEDAY

> Someday you will become an Earthquake because enough is enough!!

ANY GIVEN SOMEDAY

Someday the only ghosts will be the ugly things we say to our children
Our words go bump in the night long after they pass through our thin lips

There is no afterlife for hateful words – they are doomed to roam the winding halls of innocent minds

The things we say out loud in front of young ears can be so very sticky and haunting.

Careful. Careful. Careful.

ANY GIVEN SOMEDAY

> Someday we won't weaponize religion.

ANY GIVEN SOMEDAY

Someday we will all be beams of light chasing each other from nebula to nebula

Someday I will prove that we are so much more than what we think that we are. I don't know how I'm going to do that yet - I'm not very smart.

Let me explain:

Someday we won't be what people think about us. Someday we won't be the sum of all of our past mistakes. Someday we won't be our office jobs or the Instagram food pictures we post from a restaurant that we couldn't afford but ate there anyway or the leather seats in our car or our high school math grades. Someday we won't be any of that. I swear.

We won't even be our names. Those are just letters that

our parents tied together to make their parents happy. Someday we won't even be our bones or our skin that we spend a quarter of our life moisturizing. We aren't any of that. I'm not saying that I know what we are - I'm still working on that - slowly. It's all still a ridiculous mystery to me - to the point of paralysis. That's why I've just been sitting on park benches for ten years taking pictures of trees. Everything is a riddle to me.

Everything. Everything. Everything. This whole experience of living, for me, has been like a knotted ball of various extension cords that I have hidden in a box in my garage, so I don't have to look at it anymore. I can't move because of all this unknowing that surrounds me.

Quick question:

How have you gotten so used to being alive? It's almost like you have been through all of this before. You are a natural at it. I'm out of my element here. You know how to make money and to follow the rules while maintaining your originality while beaming your smile that makes a brilliant fall sunrise in Vermont jealous.

ANY GIVEN SOMEDAY

I'm not like you. The two of us are having different experiences here on Earth.

I'm lucky if I remember to put on underwear in the morning. I don't know how to use a semicolon or how to fix an ice maker or how to sell something on eBay or how to do anything important enough to get an award at a banquet that has a fish or beef option.

I'm forever stuck in this mystery book that you solved way back on page one. I'm not like you. I don't know anything - except:

We are more than what we have been told we are. I could be full of shit, but I believe that we are more than our contact lists or our commission checks or how clever our divorce lawyer is or our knowledge of the geopolitical tensions in Asia that we gained from reading a newspaper that somebody left on a train.

We are more than what has happened to us or what people say about us or our account balance or our Zen ankle tattoos or the poetry that I desperately write on envelopes to make you understand me or the cruise missiles we launch across borders. Come to think of it we are more than these borders that people drew hundreds of years ago to separate all of us into buckets of enemies.

We can't be any of that. None of that makes any sense to me. I think we are more than this. We have to be more. This life that we all fell into has to have more of a purpose to it.

Here is what I think:

We are light. We are energy. We are responsible for one another. We are all future spirits chasing each other from galaxy to galaxy. Someday we will be beams of light playing tag with one another.

I'll prove it. Just give me time. Like I said, I'm not very smart. I got a D- in physical science. Maybe that makes me better suited for this sort of investigation. Who knows?

If you need me I'll be in my garage untangling all of those damned extension cords.

ANY GIVEN SOMEDAY

ANY GIVEN SOMEDAY

Someday I will
be in-between being
completely gone and lingering
in front of you
like the final few notes
from a violin's love song.
I will be there -
but not really.
Like melting ice in your
fingers I will slip
from this place to the other.
For my last act I will
become the ghost
in your attic.

ANY GIVEN SOMEDAY

Someday I will
be nothing more than a
murmur in the dark,

but don't worry about
me because that is
exactly how
all great
comebacks start.

ANY GIVEN SOMEDAY

Someday
my love,
you are going
to break me
so,
you should probably
know which drawer
I keep my glue in

ANY GIVEN SOMEDAY

Someday my Depression won't have lunch with me anymore.

Someday Their Autism
Won't Scare You Anymore

listen to me,
autism is like a piece
of stained glass
autism doesn't obstruct sunlight
it changes it into a rainbow

keep listening,
autism comes through the painted glass
in a spectrum of jewel colors and with the
warmth of a constantly exploding sun.
my autistic son is a shard of that holy
glass. glowing. sacred. beautiful. burning.
unbroken. radiant.
lighting up every room he walks into

autism isn't scary
ignorance is

ANY GIVEN SOMEDAY

Someday you will be so desperate to feel normal again that you will begin to excuse the inexcusable.

Don't.

ANY GIVEN SOMEDAY

> Someday we won't keep punishing you for your brain chemistry

ANY GIVEN SOMEDAY

guidlinglight

Someday you should let yourself become an untethered kite.

Angels with wings like yours weren't meant for walking anyways
— it's a dirty business.

Give yourself permission to cut the string and to float away.

You won't be gone.
Not really.
You'll be my newest North Star.

Join the heavens.
Guide me home,
my sweet celestial body.

Someday I Will Garden With My Dad Again

buried in the soil
where my dad
used to garden
are all of my sins that he always
effortlessly pardoned

deep within this sacred peat
is where our lonely souls now meet
and just below your very lovely feet
are all the buried bones
of my redemption sweet

this dirt we share
between us
is what keeps
my soul clean
and it's
what allows me to
believe in graces
unseen

ANY GIVEN SOMEDAY

my memory has become a garden
where my dad and I go and plant
all of the words that we should have spoken
to each other - but now sadly can't

I'd say "Your grandkids look just like you
and I'm sorry that I lied."
and he'd say "I wish I could have met them
and I'm sorry that I died"

we'd shake each other's hand
and go straight back to our tasks
of gardening and forgiving each other
and sipping Jameson from a flask.

when I die and float up
to the fields past our skies
I'll be greeted with a handful of dirt
as I meet my late father's eyes

he'll say
"Come with me son, it's time for us to dig."
and I'd taste the mercy in the air and my

ANY GIVEN SOMEDAY

smile would grow so very big.

I'll grab a shovel and a bag of seed
and I'll proudly walk behind my green-
thumbed dad
wherever he may lead

ANY GIVEN SOMEDAY

Someday an internet troll will press send and instantly turn into Ash.

ANY GIVEN SOMEDAY

Someday you will
choose to stay
with me
even though
the
front door
keeps inching
closer and closer to you

Someday your dreams are going to ask you to make out for a little bit.

ANY GIVEN SOMEDAY

> SOMEDAY SUNSHINE WILL BECOME OUR GATEWAY DRUG.

Someday a hundred thousand butterflies will land and spell out the word "Surrender" on the lawn of The White House.

ANY GIVEN SOMEDAY

> Someday my first reaction will be gratitude.

Someday The Universe will stop expanding long enough for it to look back and make sure that you are keeping up with it.

ANY GIVEN SOMEDAY

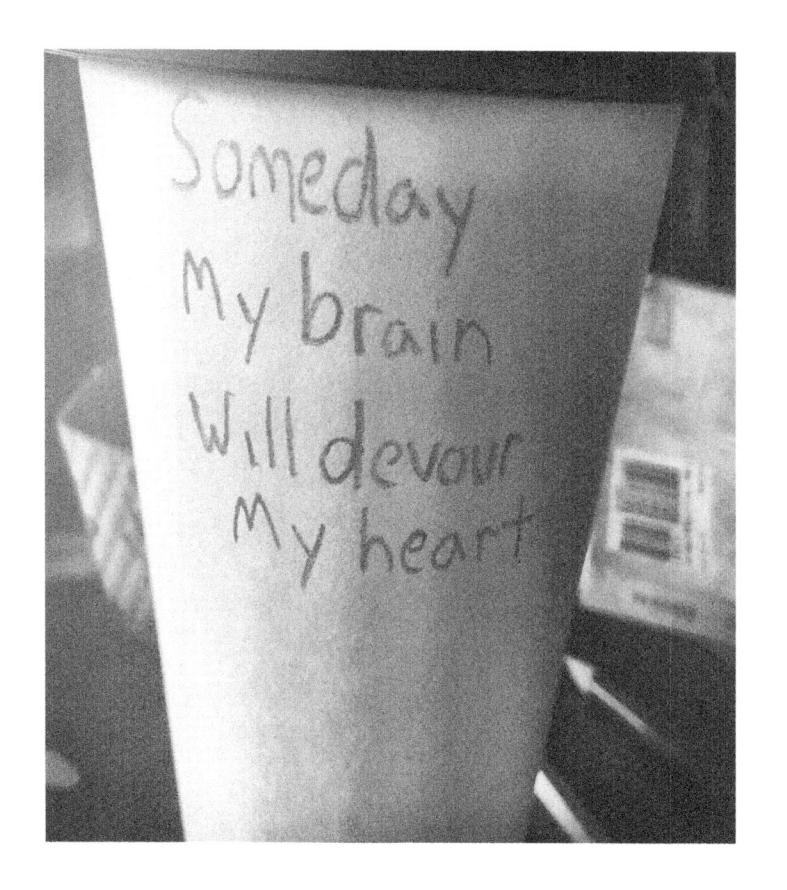

> Someday
> My brain
> Will devour
> My heart

ANY GIVEN SOMEDAY

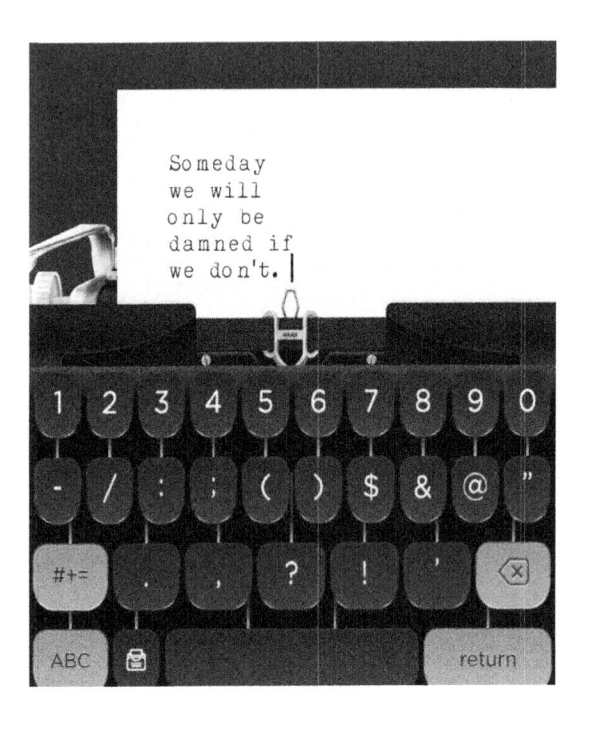

Someday
we will
only be
damned if
we don't.

Someday you will give those assholes something to really gossip about.

ANY GIVEN SOMEDAY

someday people
will be treated
with more dignity
than guns.

ANY GIVEN SOMEDAY

> Someday you will finally forgive me and I will turn into a Rosebush.

Someday

        indifference

won't

            be sexy.

Someday love will hurt you, but it will never shame you. If it does, it wasn't love in the first place. Love can bite – but it should never chew.

Someday we will turn all of our scars into violin strings

ANY GIVEN SOMEDAY

> Someday grief won't be confused with nostalgia.

Someday we will quit making our common ground so sacred that we never ever visit it.

ANY GIVEN SOMEDAY

> Someday you
> will be kissed
> so softly that
> your lips
> will turn into
> falling
> cotton

ANY GIVEN SOMEDAY

i.

Someday when I write our story I'm going to make sure that we meet each other sooner.

ii.

Someday I'm going to replace all of your mirrors with paintings of beautiful sunflowers.

iii.

Someday you'll have to choose between being the dragon or being the treasure.

> Someday my sins will just be called my backstory.

ANY GIVEN SOMEDAY

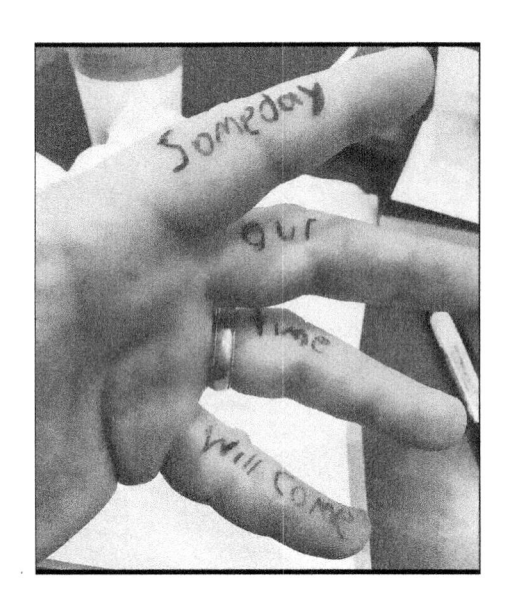

Someday there will be more clean drinking water than ammo.

Someday silence will never be considered
a ***treatment.***

ANY GIVEN SOMEDAY

> Someday I will hollow you out just to make sure that you'll always have room for me.

Someday I won't be surprised to discover that heaven is just you in a new sundress standing in an open field under a blanket of ancient stars.

ANY GIVEN SOMEDAY

> Someday hope will be the third act plot twist

ANY GIVEN SOMEDAY

someday you will
give your heart to
somebody and they
won't grind it into a
blade to stab you with

instead they will
wrap your heart
up in a lavender
soaked garment
and lay it in the great
spring rush until it's
polished into a smooth
crimson river rock

don't believe the poets
love isn't the heart that cuts

love is the heart that skips
love doesn't bleed you out

love walks with you on the water

ANY GIVEN SOMEDAY

> Someday
> Can you
> show me
> what you
> were like
> before I
> ruined you?

ANY GIVEN SOMEDAY

Someday my memories won't smell like Red Ropes Licorice

Open up a bag of
Red Ropes Licorice
And suddenly I'm
Eight years old again.

It's 1982.
I'm standing in
The middle of
Our family's drug store.
The waxy floors
That are only cleaned
Every six weeks.
The humming lights
That never quite illuminate
The corners of the open space.

The bins of kite string
And rows of Russell Stovers chocolate.
The birthstone jewelry counter
And the smell of raw film

ANY GIVEN SOMEDAY

Coming from the camera department.

I'm back.
Really.
This isn't a dream.
I can feel the bag of licorice
against my hairless arms.
I swear.
It's my wormhole to the past.
Please believe me.

I can see my dad
Behind the pharmacy counter
Smiling
Always smiling
Handing a red-haired
Man a bottle of eggshell pills.

At this age I don't really know what a pharmacist does. People bring in slips of paper with the worst handwriting you would ever see and give them to my father so he can transform them into amber colored vials. He is a magician.

The red-haired

ANY GIVEN SOMEDAY

Man leaves and
My dad raises
His hand to
His mouth and
Takes a long
Drag from his
Cigarette.
A cigarette that he
got from our store.
We have as much
tobacco in stock
As we did any medicine
That was used to fight it.

Our store sold both
The disease and the cure.

My dad, with
A haze of
Cancer around him
Finds me with his eyes.

I am sixty feet away
I am 35 years away

ANY GIVEN SOMEDAY

But
I am caught in his gaze
Like a fish on a line.
My dad smiles at me.
I am complete.
I live for his smile.
He is my hero.

He begins to fade
Into the smoke.
The store is disappearing
I am traveling back.
Before he is obscured
And I'm returned to
My uncomfortable adulthood,
I smile at my dad one last time
As he does at me.
As he does at me.
As he does at me.

We are now shadows to one another.
I take to my Red Ropes.
My dad takes to his smoking.
I'm back.

ANY GIVEN SOMEDAY

The vision is over.
Every time I eat red licorice
I can still smell the
smoke and see his incandescent smile.
cancer can't
Kill our memories.
So, I think
That makes it powerless.

**

"punchlines"

someday I will
tell you the
joke about the
man who was too
afraid to open
knocking doors.

It's not a
particularly funny
joke.

Someday I am going to replace all the mirrors in your house with paintings of beautiful sunflowers, so you will finally see you the exact same way that I do.

ANY GIVEN SOMEDAY

Someday when you no longer believe in God anymore, I will ask you to go put your naked feet into the river where your daddy used to take you fishing as a child.
  The cold moving water will contain a memory that you have long forgotten. It will come back to you through the sounds of the gossiping pines and lapping water.

There in the middle of the river you will remember the soft words that your daddy used to say to you while tying up all your fishing lines:
"You are so lovely.
You are so loved.
You are my love.
You are as pretty and as rare
as any wildflower that has ever existed."
If you ever want proof of God just investigate the river water passing through your bare toes. You are the proof of the divine that you have been looking for this whole time.
You are the proof.

Stand in the water until you remember.

ANY GIVEN SOMEDAY

Someday you will be sitting in a hard wooden chair answering hard wooden questions being asked by hard wooden people.

In that moment I want you to remember that you are made of silk.

Someday all of
the words that we
are too afraid
to say to each
other will be
the only thing
that fill
up the space
between us.

ANY GIVEN SOMEDAY

Someday it won't be your politics that Divide us.

It will be your hate.

ANY GIVEN SOMEDAY

Someday a coma patient
will wake up and her first
question won't be "What did
I miss?" Instead she will
ask her gathering family
 "Did you miss me?"

Nobody will know how to answer that.

Someday when you aren't okay, you will need to look me in the eyes and tell me. I probably won't be able to notice on my own. Sorry. Just grab me by my hands and speak your pain to me so very slowly.

You may have to yell – *my narcissism is hard of hearing.*

ANY GIVEN SOMEDAY

someday
a person
will call
you "Sweet Baby"
and you will
walk straight
out of the fucking
door without saying
another word because you are
the opposite of helpless.

You are a supernova
with a smile.

You aren't sweet.
You are the river
of salt and rage
and wildflowers
and passion
and jagged rocks
and life without apologies.
You are zero ebb
and all flow.

You ain't nobody's
Sweet Baby.

You are the fury.

Someday isn't here yet. Be right here with me in this wonderful now. I know you're leaving me tomorrow. Please quit mentioning it. I know that these are our last moments together before you get on that bus.

Please stop talking about the future.

The frozen air between us is like dragon fire smoke. The smell of fresh snowfall and the sound of your pink and white jacket crinkling. Hold my hand for warmth. No, wait - it's for more than that. Hold my hand forever. Is that too weird to hear me say? Here is what you should know: I am never as strong as I am when I am weakly lying in your arms.

The wind is here now. Your tears are freezing on your soft skin. Quit talking about someday. It's not here yet...

I hate the word "**yet**". It's a tease. It's more than a tease – it's more ominous than that. It's always the dramatic last plot twist in a sentence.

Dinner's not ready.... **yet**.

The master assassin doesn't want to kill you just...**yet**.

The cancer isn't going away.... yet.

Some people think that **yet**
Is a hopeful word.
Like something good is on its way.

ANY GIVEN SOMEDAY

I don't see it like that.
For me, **yet** is the monster hidden under our bed.
My yet is always half empty and half full of
Gypsy-cursed urine.
Yet is always the other shoe that needs to drop.
How many more shoes can there be?

Wait - where are we? Oh yes. We are right here. In
the snow.

Let's just enjoy this moment.
This perfect now.
Frosted lips on frosted lips.
Hands desperately being held.
Snow in our head.
This perfect now.
Tomorrow isn't here.
Just this fire between us.
That's all there is.
Quit talking about leaving.

Quit talking about breaking my heart
It's not tomorrow...

ANY GIVEN SOMEDAY

It's not someday...
Not just **yet**.
yet yet yet yet yet

I fucking hate that word.
Why cant I stop using it?
Let's go inside.
I am getting cold.

don't leave
me just
yet

Someday a gardener with sharp clippers will come across a bright yellow dandelion that can speak.

ANY GIVEN SOMEDAY

The gardener will kneel beside the dandelion, so he can hear its soft song-songy voice.

"Don't hurt me, the dandelion will start. "I'm a flower. I'm beautiful. I have a light inside. I'm not afraid of you. I'm a miracle. Please, let me show you.

The gardener will smile. The shaking dandelion will smile back.

"I'm a flower," the dandelion will whisper just as the clippers decapitate it.

"I get to decide what a flower is," the gardener will say as he looks around for his next victim.

Someday
    everything that

ANY GIVEN SOMEDAY

is wrong with me
won't be used
against us.

Someday a pigeon will fly

ANY GIVEN SOMEDAY

into an enormous hurricane and it will come out the
other side as a dove.

And on that particular
someday, nobody will see the
transformation take place because nobody
believes in miracles
anymore.

Oh, God, send me
a hurricane and let me
become a dove.

ANY GIVEN SOMEDAY

Someday I will
be in-between being
completely gone and lingering
in front of you
like the final few notes
from a violin's love song.
I will be there -
but not really.
Like melting ice in your
fingers I will slip
from this place to the other.
For my last act I will
become the ghost
in your attic.

god >

Text Message
Today 10:35 AM

Someday a comet will decide to spare at the very last second because two lovers will kiss goodbye under its glowing blue tail

Not Delivered

Someday God, will you please quit lighting me on fire while asking me to remain patient?

Not Delivered

Someday I'm afraid that the rain will make our children sick.

Not Delivered

Please write me back.

Not Delivered

ANY GIVEN SOMEDAY

Someday a brave little boy will close his eyes and the hands that are choking him will turn into a bluebird that will fly away.

Someday they will
 ask you to
settle and you'll

never stop laughing.

ANY GIVEN SOMEDAY

> Someday I will go out of my mind but I'll have to come right back because I won't have anywhere else to go.

ANY GIVEN SOMEDAY

ANY GIVEN SOMEDAY

> Someday
> I
> won't have to
> write
> on top
> of coffee
> stains
> again.

ANY GIVEN SOMEDAY

Someday you will lace my hands so tightly in yours that I will become your old comfortable shoe.

This Isn't About Weakness

Someday these tears won't feel like bullets loaded into the chamber of a gun anymore. They will feel like delicate blue eggs about to hatch. My tears will smell like vanilla French toast on the griddle.

My tears will be a salty waterfall of all the sunshine and all of the thunder and all of the courage and all of the grace and all of the redemption that has ever existed. Every tear will carry the unmistakable DNA of how I survived hidden in them.

Someday a robot will be asked to cry to prove that it has a soul because is there any other way to figure that out?

ANY GIVEN SOMEDAY

Someday instead of shaking at the start of a conversation we will just rest our palms on each other's cheeks.

Someday when our souls leave our bodies our spirits will float up to heaven on every single tear that we have ever produced.

Someday my tears will sing "Amazing Grace" while they pour down my cracked and wrinkled face.

Someday we won't cry when relationships end, but rather at the very moment they begin.

Someday the best lesson you will ever learn will come from a single fat daddy teardrop on the bridge of your nose.

This isn't about weakness.

ANY GIVEN SOMEDAY

> someday you'll vote your heart and not your party

I think I lost
you the moment
that you started
to fall in love
with winning

can I tell you something?

there is no winning
because there has

ANY GIVEN SOMEDAY

never been anything
to win

there are no medal ceremonies
there are no jackpots
there are no boardwalks with hotels
there are no bullseyes

relax,
there isn't a game
that you need to win
there is only us
and the holy delicate
strings that
we tie between each
other to keep us
floating up into oblivion
I'll say it again
we are tied to each other
we are laced up
together by
common strings

how can you win that sort of game?

ANY GIVEN SOMEDAY

there is only
us and the way
we help each other
survive between sunsets
it's not a race
it never was
we are all tortoises
ambling down
the same track
together toward
the same
finish line
of eternity

there is nothing to win

but if you aren't careful
there is everything to lose
so don't ignore the itch under
your skin telling you there
is more to this organic ride
than just winning
there is community
there is healing
there is us

ANY GIVEN SOMEDAY

there are the ties
that bind us to one another
winning won't
welcome you
on your first day
in the great beyond

but I will

please listen,

it's time to start listening
to your heart again

it's not too late

I swear

I'm tugging at our common strings

Can't you feel it?

ANY GIVEN SOMEDAY

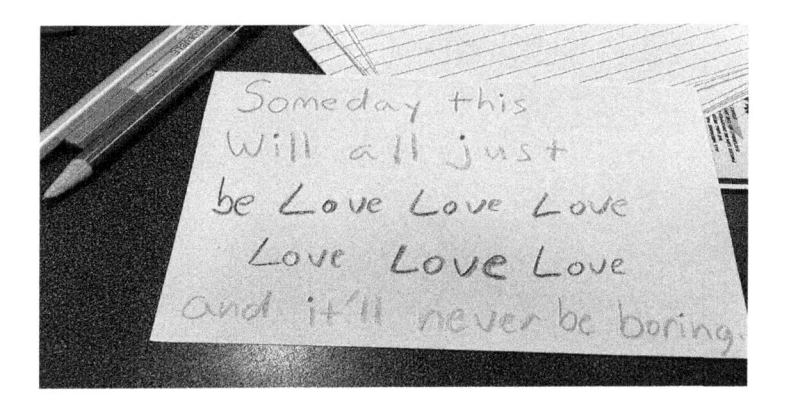

> Someday this will all just be Love Love Love Love Love Love and it'll never be boring.

ANY GIVEN SOMEDAY

Someday you will kiss somebody
 with your eyes wide open and it will
 be the bravest thing
 you have ever done.

SOMEDAY A STRAY CAT ON YOUR FRONT PORCH WILL MAKE YOU BELIEVE IN REINCARNATION.

ANY GIVEN SOMEDAY

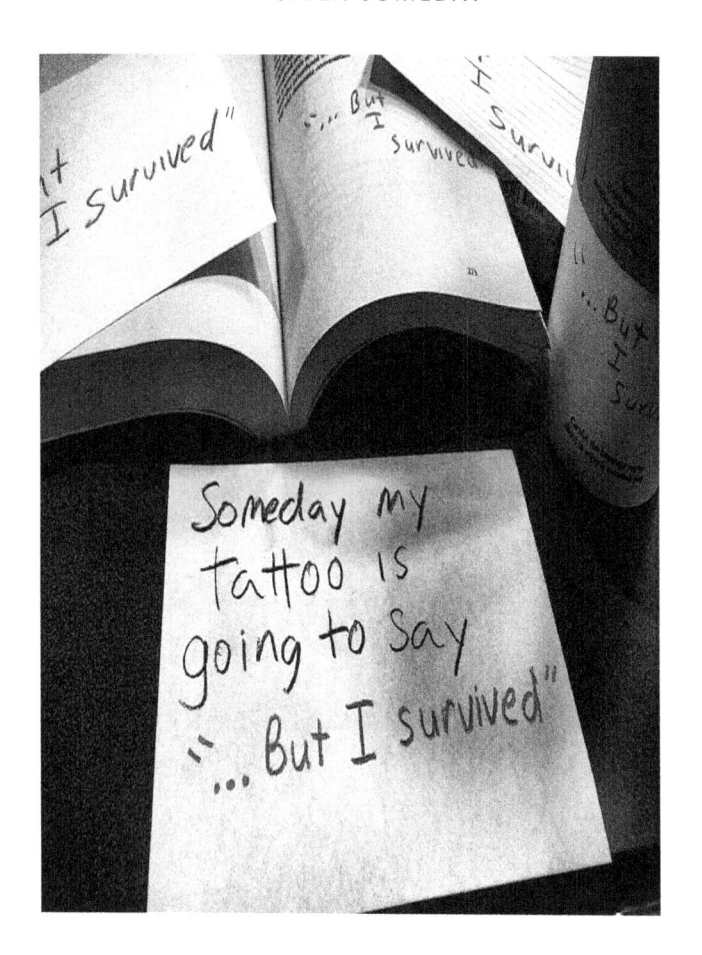

About The Author:

John Roedel is a Wyoming based writer who is trying his best.

Recently he published his first book "Hey God. Hey John. : What Happens When God Writes Back." about his complicated relationship with the divine.

For more information on John please visit his webpage
heygodheyjohn.com

Printed in Great Britain
by Amazon